THE WOW AND THE HOW

PLANET EARTH

ANNABELLE LYNCH

Gareth Stevens
PUBLISHING

Please visit our website, www.garethstevens.com. For a free color catalog of all our high-quality books, call toll free 1-800-542-2595 or fax 1-877-542-2596.

Cataloging-in-Publication Data
Names: Lynch, Annabelle.
Title: Planet Earth / Annabelle Lynch.
Description: Buffalo, NY : Gareth Stevens Publishing, 2026. | Series: The wow and the how | Includes glossary and index.
Identifiers: ISBN 9781482473094 (pbk.) | ISBN 9781482473100 (library bound) | ISBN 9781482473117 (ebook)
Subjects: LCSH: Earth (Planet)--Juvenile literature.
Classification: LCC QB631.4 L963 2026 | DDC 525--dc23

Published in 2026 by
Gareth Stevens Publishing
2544 Clinton St.
Buffalo, NY 14224

First published in Great Britain in 2024 by Hodder & Stoughton

Authors: Paul Rockett, Victoria Brooker, Amy Pimperton, Julia Bird, Grace Glendinning, Elise Short, Melanie Palmer

Series designer: Rocket Design (East Anglia) Ltd

Picture credits:
Shutterstock: Amiak f cover bg, Angkrit b cover bl, 3tr, 19c, Aphelleon/elements of this image furnished by NASA 10-11bg, BlueRingMedia f cover tr, b cover tr, 1tr, 4tl, 9c, 11b, 23c, 24r, 29c, BNP Design Studio b cover tl, Willyam Bradberry 26-27 main, Catalyst Labs f cover br, 1b, 8tr, Colorfuel Studio 5bl, Curioso Photography 20-21bg, Damsea 18-19bg, Deeg 28b,Mikhail Dudarev 6-7bg, Prihanto Edi 11c, Escova 18cl,18br, Foodonwhite 18tl, Freedom100m 29b, Gdvcom 21b, GN Studio 22bl, Goinyk Production 28-29bg,Hendrikk7 3tl, 9b,v.iraa 5tr, Johavel 20b, Lelia Ledencova 8-9bg, Ron Leishman 11t, light_s 13b,Ekaterina Mikhaylova 7t, liu_miu 21t, Naeblys 12, 24l, Nosyrevy 27bl, Npeter f cover c, 1c, 4-5c, 8c, Oleg and Polly 4tr, ONYXprj 2-3b, 22-23b,Owatta 10b, PegaSu Studio 27r, 30, Photopictures 7b, RJC Cartoons 6b,Andrew Rybalko 16b, Sabelskaya 31, Amy Sachar 25c, Sararoom Design 13c, 25b, Amanita Silvicora 5c, Andrey Suslov 19b, SvetlanaARTdreams 10c, Tinkivinki 6c, Tn-prints 4cl, Volodymyr Tverdokhlib 13t, twobears_art 17b,VectorVicePhoto 18cr, Yaroslav Vitkovskiy 22-23bg,Vixit 16t, Vladimirat 14,White Space Illustrations 15c, Wink Images 4b, 5br, Tatyana Yamshanova 22t.

All additional design elements from Shutterstock or drawn by designer.

Printed in the United States of America

CPSIA compliance information: Batch #CSGS26: For further information contact Gareth Stevens at 1-800-542-2595.

CONTENTS

THE WOW OF EARTH!

Our planet Earth is AMAZING! It is the only planet in the known universe that has plants and animals–including us–living on it. WOW!

We are able to live on Earth because of **HOW** it was formed. It has water that we can drink, air we can breathe, and plants that we can eat.

Our planet also contains many other wonders, such as rivers, mountains, and forests. We may think we know how rivers flow and mountains grow but some facts need more exploration.

Discover amazing facts about Earth including some that may challenge what you thought you knew. Find out the science behind these world wonders to understand how our planet Earth works. Can you find your own **WOW** facts about Earth?

WOW! Earth was once a single supercontinent!

About every 450 million years, tectonic plates break up, separate and then come together again to form one massive supercontinent.

HOW?

Underneath the ground, there are massive, moving pieces of rock called tectonic plates. These plates move around and bump into each other and cause volcanoes, mountains, and earthquakes.

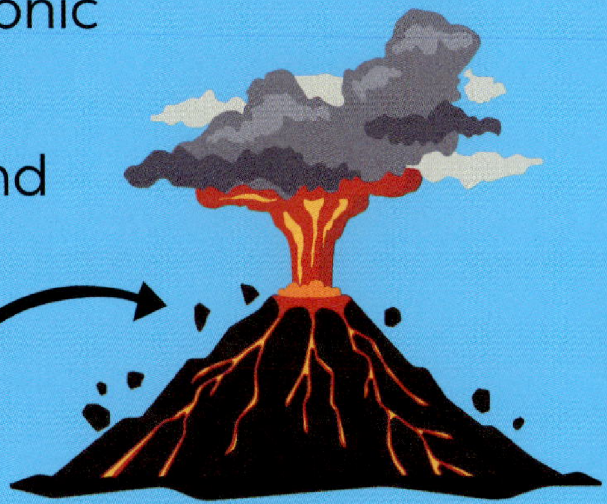

A long time ago, these tectonic plates came together to make one large land mass – a supercontinent! Then they gradually drifted apart to make separate continents as we know them today.

AMAZING EARTH

Most tectonic plates move 2 to 4 inches (5 to 10 cm) per year. Scientists suggest that the next supercontinent will form 250 million years from now.

WOW! Earth isn't round!

EARTH HAS NEVER BEEN PERFECTLY ROUND. OUR PLANET IS WIDER AT THE EQUATOR THAN AT THE POLES.

HOW?

The planet bulges around the equator because of Earth's rotation. This variation is too tiny to be seen in pictures of Earth from space, so the planet appears round to the human eye.

In fact, the shape of Earth is always changing. Sometimes this change is due to the daily tides, or to the drift of tectonic plates, and sometimes it is due to events such as earthquakes, volcanic eruptions, or meteor strikes.

AMAZING EARTH

Recent research suggests that melting glaciers are causing Earth's middle to spread. Gravity pushes extra masses of water and earth into a bulge around our planet.

WOW!

A year on Earth isn't 365 days!

IN FACT, A YEAR IS 365 DAYS, 5 HOURS, 48 MINUTES AND 46 SECONDS.

SUN

EARTH

Weeee!

HOW?

A year is the time it takes Earth to orbit (go around) the sun once. It actually takes Earth 365 and ¼ days to orbit the sun. So, every four years, we have a leap year that adds up the four extra quarters to make a whole day. This extra day is February 29.

If we never had a leap year, over time a summer month would be a winter month! Brrr ...

AMAZING EARTH

We also round up the length of a day. A day really takes 23 hours, 56 minutes and 4 seconds.

WOW!

Earth's core is as hot as the sun!

EXPERTS THINK THAT PART OF EARTH'S CORE IS ABOUT THE SAME TEMPERATURE AS THE SURFACE OF THE SUN.

HOW?

Earth's core is the very center of our planet. It is made up of the outer core and inner core. The inner core is a hot ball of solid metal. The outer core is made up mostly of liquid metals, iron, and nickel. Between these two is where the temperature is the hottest.

After the core, Earth's next layer is a bit cooler and is called the mantle. It's made of liquid rock, which escapes as lava when a volcano erupts.

Earth cools further as you get nearer to the surface layer, called the crust.

AMAZING EARTH

The core is about the size of a dwarf planet, like Pluto.

WOW!

48 volcanoes are erupting right NOW!

THERE ARE **1,350** ACTIVE VOLCANOES IN THE WORLD TODAY THAT ARE LIKELY TO ERUPT NOW OR IN THE FUTURE.

AMAZING EARTH

Most of the world's volcanoes are found around the RING OF FIRE, a chain of volcanoes that surrounds the Pacific Ocean.

HOW?

A volcano is an opening in Earth's crust from which melted rock, ash, and gases are forced out in an eruption. An active volcano means one that could erupt again. Inside an active volcano is a chamber where molten rock, called magma, collects. Pressure builds up inside the chamber and eventually causes the magma to break out of the ground.

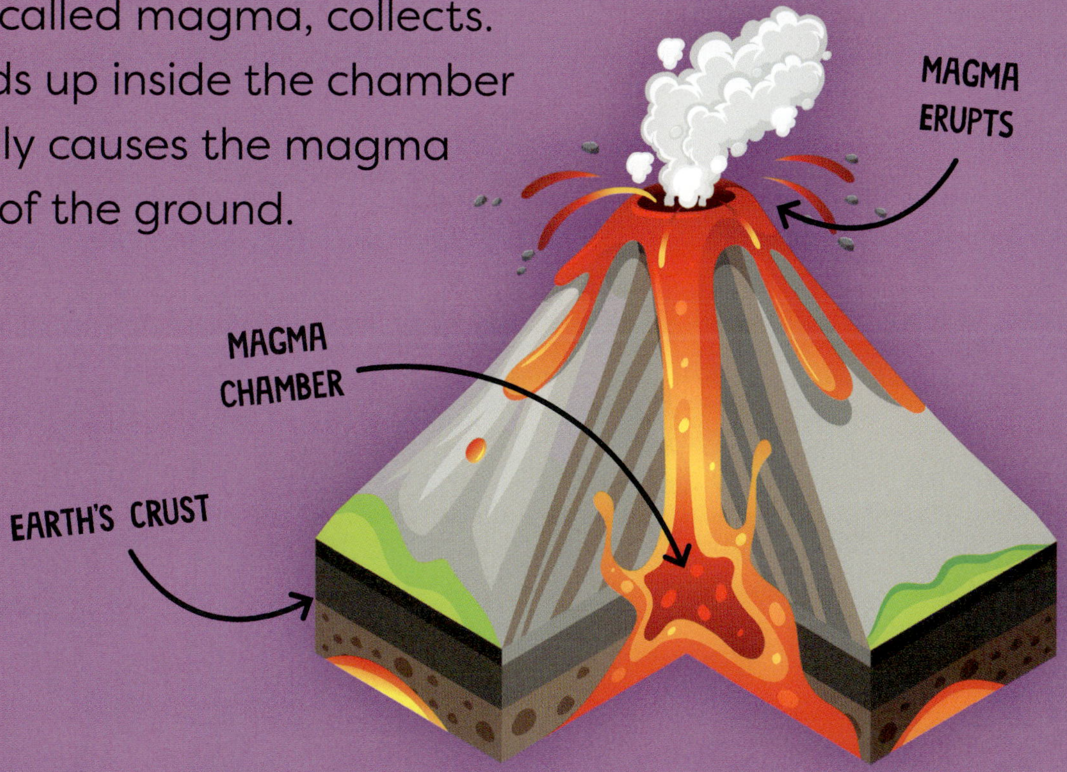

Not all volcanic eruptions are life-threatening. Eruptions can vary from a gentle oozing to explosive blasts. Some volcanoes continually erupt during the year. Stromboli, off the coast of Italy, has been erupting almost continuously for most of the past 2,000 years!

WOW! Mountains can grow and shrink!

The ninth highest mountain on Earth, Nanga Parbat, part of the Himalayan mountains in Asia, is one of the fastest growing, at a rate of 0.3 inch (7 mm) per year.

HOW?

Mountains are formed when the tectonic plates that cover the surface of Earth meet and one plate slips under the other, causing the land to rise. As the land rises, mountains are formed. Tectonic plates are always moving and so one plate can continue to move under the other, known as tectonic uplift, pushing the mountain up higher.

Weather, such as strong winds or rain, frozen as well as running water, eat away at the surface and peaks of mountains causing them to shrink in height. The action and impact of the weather is a process known as erosion.

AMAZING EARTH

Some mountains grow and shrink in equal measure at the same time. This means that they neither get taller or shorter as both processes cancel out any gain or loss in height.

WOW!

80 percent of the ocean is unexplored!

WATER MAY COVER MOST OF EARTH'S SURFACE, BUT WHAT ACTUALLY LIES BENEATH OUR OCEANS REMAINS A (DEEP) MYSTERY.

HOW?

Oceanographers have a very tough job exploring the ocean floor. For one thing, it's dark down there. Really dark! When you dive 650 feet (200 m) below the surface it gets pretty murky. Below 3,280 feet (1,000 m) it's completely black and this can extend farther. The lack of sunlight also means it's extremely cold.

Strange creatures lurk in the depths ...

Most challenging of all is the pressure of the water above you. This pressure increases the deeper you go. At the oceans' deepest point, the Mariana Trench, the pressure is an eye-popping 1,000 times greater than at the surface. (No wonder oceanographers rely on expensive, high-tech submersibles to explore the oceans safely.)

AMAZING EARTH

NASA is researching the ocean floor as they believe that conditions there are similar to those on other planets (and will help them with their research without having to travel into space).

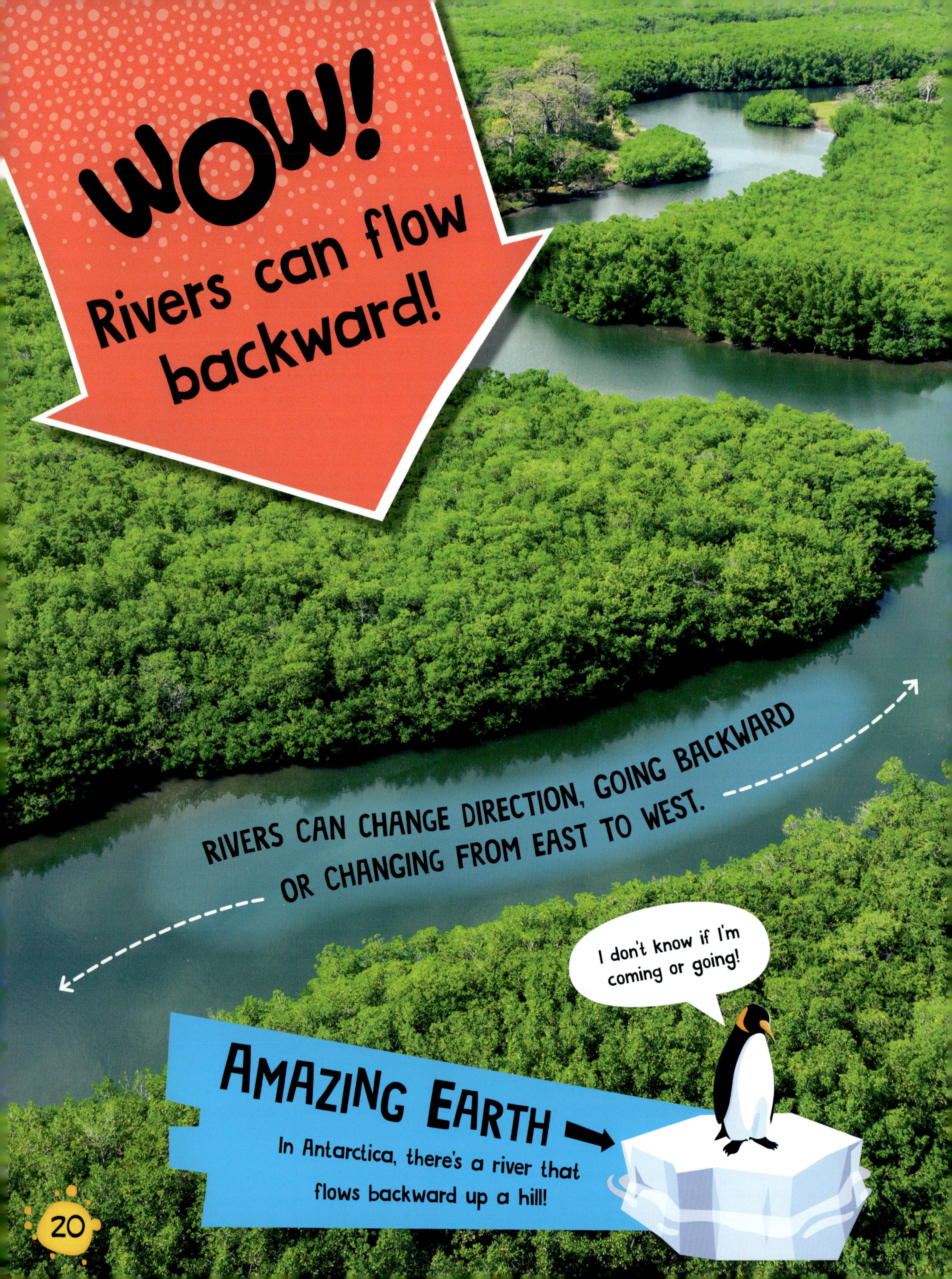

WOW!

Rivers can flow backward!

RIVERS CAN CHANGE DIRECTION, GOING BACKWARD OR CHANGING FROM EAST TO WEST.

AMAZING EARTH

In Antarctica, there's a river that flows backward up a hill!

HOW?

In 2012 and 2021, passing hurricanes made the Mississippi River flow backward. The force of the winds caused the river water to move incredibly fast but in the wrong direction. Over 100 years before that, a powerful earthquake caused a dam in the river to form, which also pushed the water backward.

The Mississippi isn't the only river where this has happened. Sometimes rivers are reversed to stop pollution or to change the shape of the land so towns can be built. The Chicago River's flow was deliberately reversed to stop polluted water from reaching towns and cities.

The Chicago River

WOW! Earth's tides are caused by the moon!

WHEN THE MOON ORBITS AROUND EARTH IT CAUSES THE OCEANS TO BULGE OUT AT EITHER SIDE.

HOW?

Gravity is a force that keeps us on Earth and stops us from floating up into space. The bigger the object, the bigger the pulling force that gravity has on objects around it. The Earth and moon have a gravitational pull on each other. This is what stops the moon from flying out of its orbit around Earth. As the moon travels around Earth, its gravitational pull causes the ocean to bulge out. It pulls at the oceans causing the tides to rise at either side of Earth.

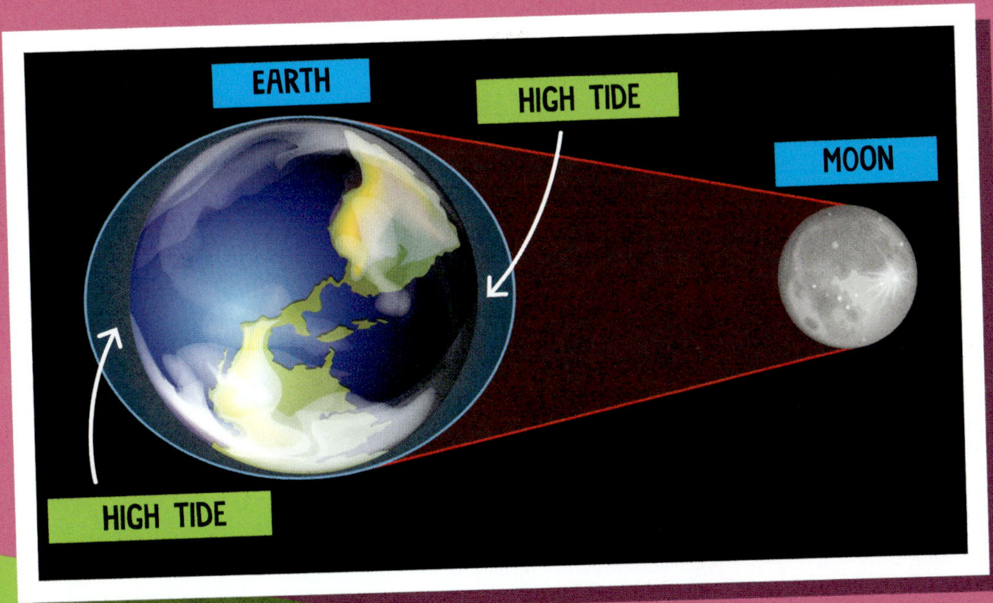

AMAZING EARTH

Tides are at their highest during a new moon or a full moon. This happens when the sun, Earth, and moon are positioned in a line together and have a greater combined force of gravity that has a stronger pull on the oceans. These are known as spring tides.

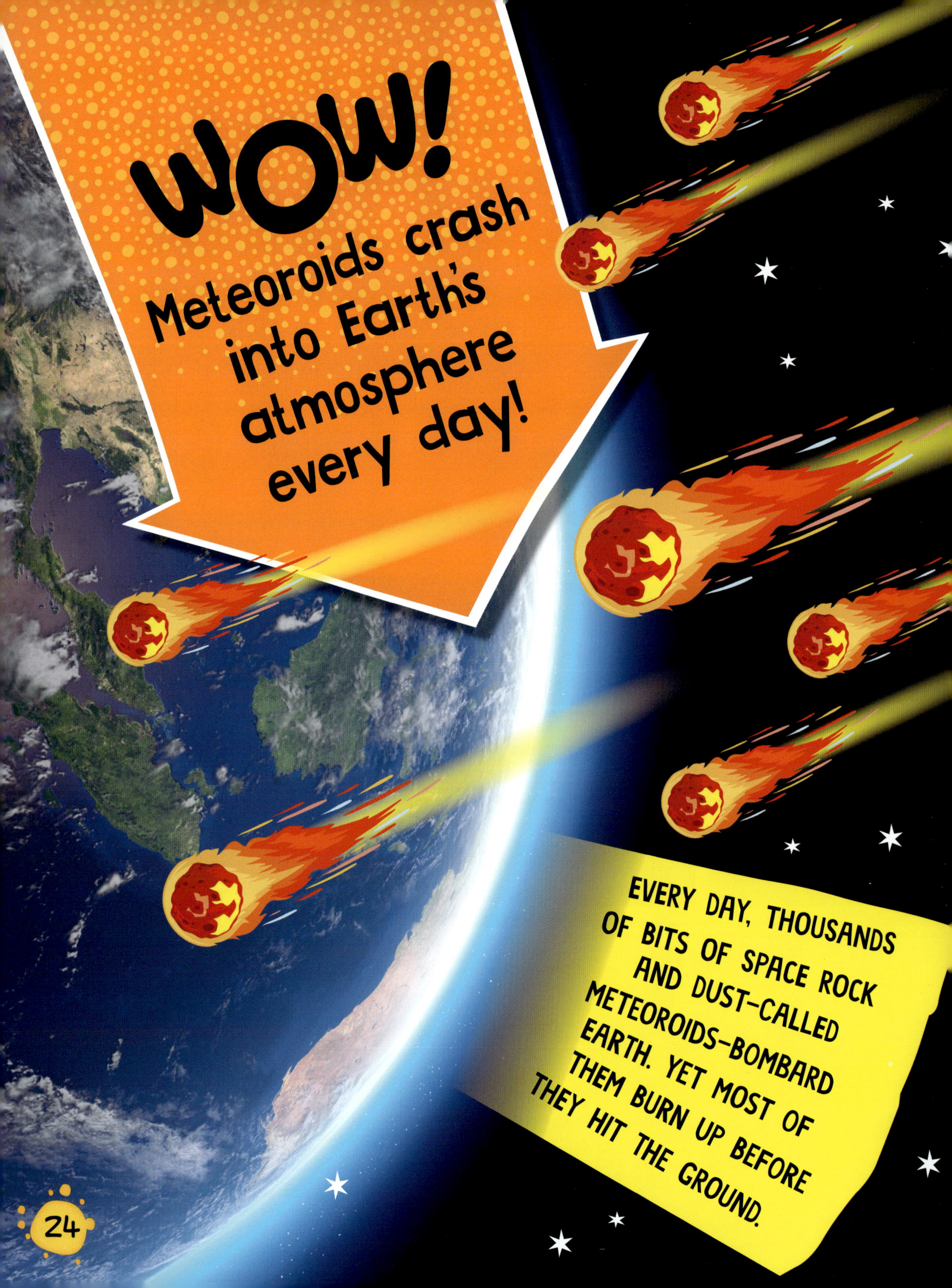

WOW!

Meteoroids crash into Earth's atmosphere every day!

EVERY DAY, THOUSANDS OF BITS OF SPACE ROCK AND DUST—CALLED METEOROIDS—BOMBARD EARTH. YET MOST OF THEM BURN UP BEFORE THEY HIT THE GROUND.

HOW?

Earth's atmosphere is made of matter–mostly gases with dust particles. When a meteoroid hits Earth's atmosphere at speeds of up to 161,060 miles (259,200 km) per hour, it rubs against the matter. This creates friction, which causes a meteoroid to heat up and burn. The light we see streaking across the sky as it burns is called a meteor or shooting star.

On average, only 17 meteoroids hit Earth's surface each day. These rocks are then called meteorites.

AMAZING EARTH

The chances of being hit by a meteorite are tiny as most land in the ocean or on uninhabited land. It's the huge "dinosaur killer" asteroids we need to worry about!

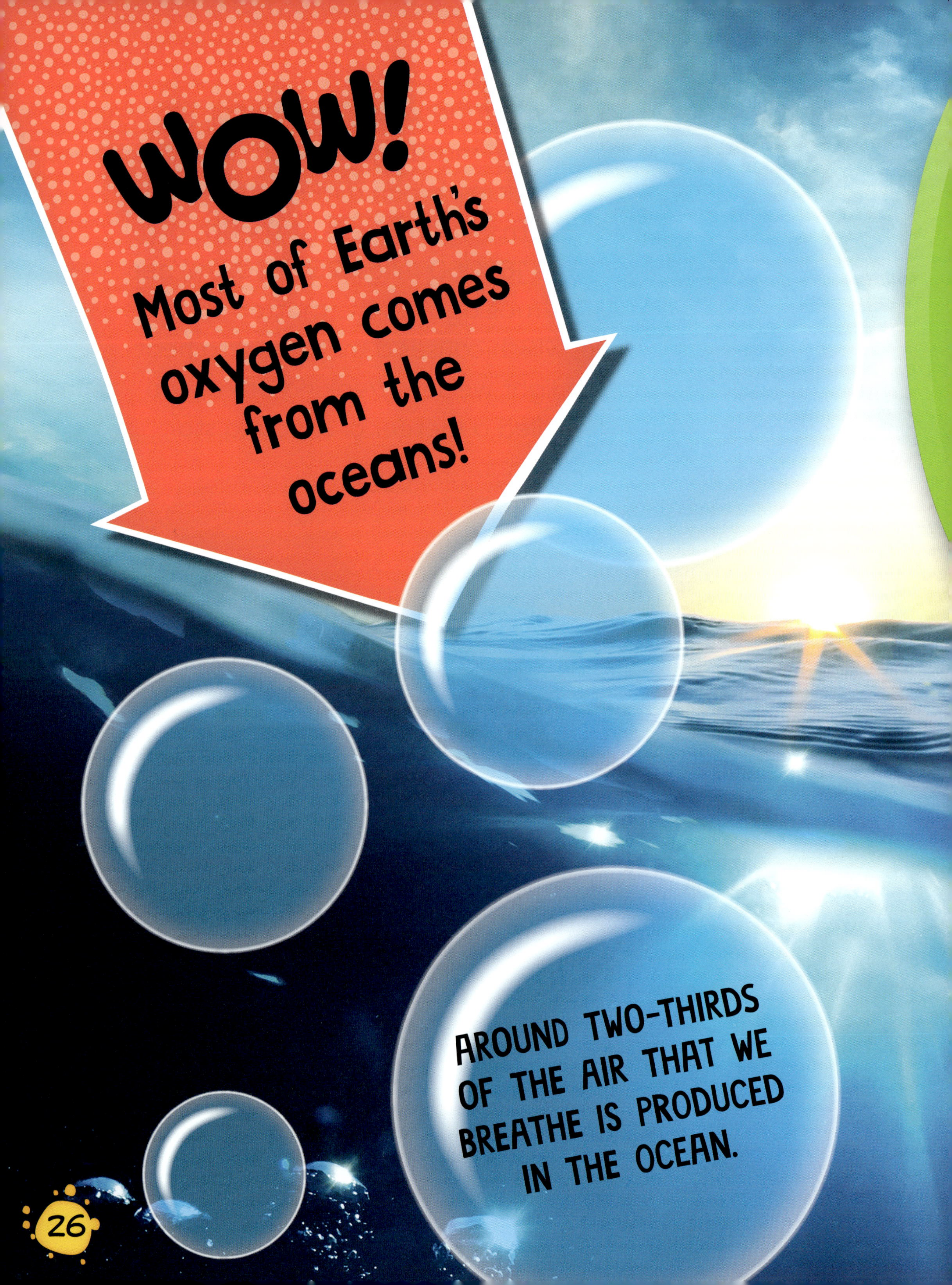

WOW!

Most of Earth's oxygen comes from the oceans!

AROUND TWO-THIRDS OF THE AIR THAT WE BREATHE IS PRODUCED IN THE OCEAN.

HOW?

It's actually the plants and trillions of tiny plant-like organisms called phytoplankton that live in ocean water that produce most of the air we breathe. By the process of photosynthesis, they take energy from sunlight and turn a gas called carbon dioxide into sugar and oxygen. They then eat the sugar and release the oxygen into the atmosphere.

Trees on land create their share of oxygen too. They produce around a fifth of the world's oxygen. And the bigger the tree, the more oxygen it emits.

AMAZING EARTH

Some scientists say that a tiny phytoplankton provides the oxygen for one in every five breaths we take.

WOW!
Antarctica is the largest desert in the world!
IT MIGHT NOT HAVE ANY SAND, BUT IT'S KNOWN AS A DESERT BECAUSE IT'S SO DRY!
GASP!
We're really thirsty but everything is frozen solid.
It's cold too!

HOW?

Not all deserts are hot and sandy. A desert is a place that gets less than 10 inches (250 mm) of rain or snow a year. Even though Antarctica is basically just ice and snow, it doesn't get much new rain or snow. In fact, some parts of Antarctica get less than 2 inches (50 mm) of rain or snow each year. It's possible that certain parts have not had rain in the past 14 million years!

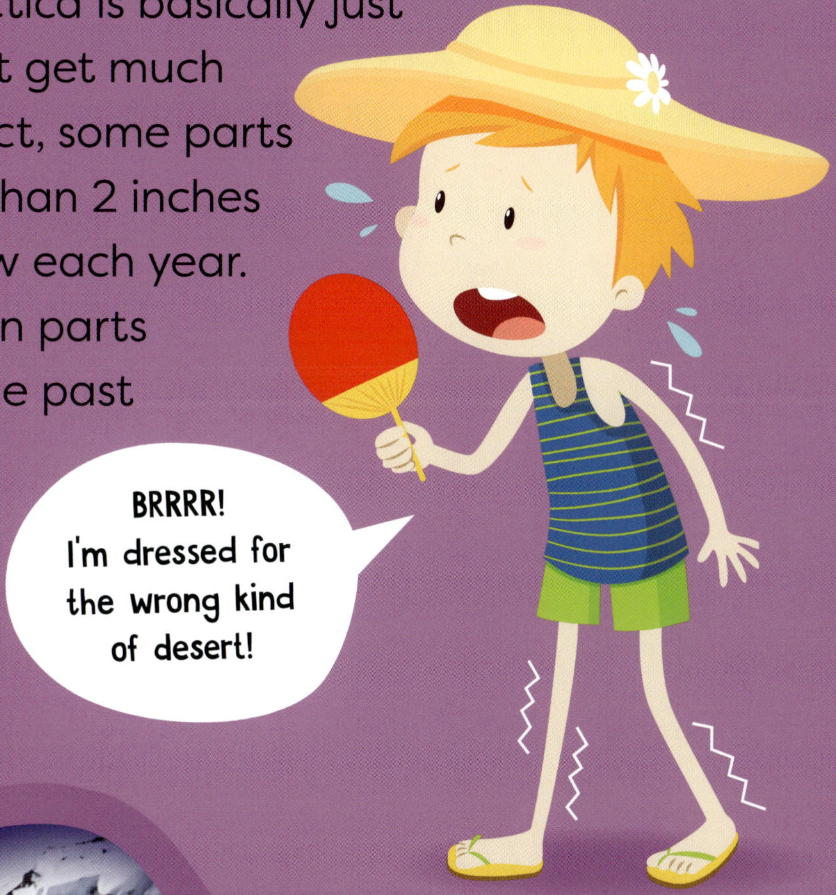

AMAZING EARTH

The Sahara is the largest hot desert in the world. Rain is very rare but when it does come, it's usually a huge downpour that can cause floods!

Glossary

atmosphere the gases that surround Earth

equator the imaginary circle around Earth that is halfway between the North and South Poles

gravity the force by which all objects in the universe are attracted to each other

oceanographer someone who studies or maps the ocean and the animals and plants that live there

pollution waste or other materials that damage the environment

pressure a force

tectonic plates large pieces of moving rock which form Earth's crust

tides the flow of water away from or back to the land

Further Reading

Books

Fact or Fake: The Truth about Planet Earth
by Sonya Newland (Wayland, 2022)

Into the Volcano: The Science, Magic, and Meaning of Volcanoes
by Cath Ard (Flying Eye Books, 2024)

STEM in the Ocean
by Megan Borgert-Spaniol (Checkerboard Library, 2024)

Websites

www.bbcearth.com/bbc-earth-kids
Everything you ever wanted to know about Earth.

www.natgeokids.com/uk/discover/science/space/facts-about-the-earth/
Fun facts about Earth.

https://www.planetsforkids.org/planet-earth.html
Find out about the formation and structure of Earth.

INDEX